The Wildlife Conservation Society saves wildlife and wild lands. We do so through careful science, international conservation, education, and the management of the world's largest system of urban wildlife parks, led by the flagship Bronx Zoo. Together, these activities change individual attitudes towards nature and help people imagine wildlife and humans living in sustainable interaction on both a local and global scale. WCS is committed to this work because we believe it essential to the integrity of life on Earth.

All images are copyright of the Wildlife Conservation Society developed in conjunction with Young and Rubicam, and designed by Stuart Garrett and Ted McCagg. Expert readers for this book were Don Moore and Bruce Foster.
Photo credits:
Gorilla, Rhino, Ibis, Okapi, Langur: Dennis DeMello
Caiman: Jim Tamarack
Cobra: Bill Meng
Spot illustrations by David Neuhaus.

ISBN 0-439-41918-2

12  11                                                                11 12 13 14/0

Printed in the U.S.A.
First Scholastic printing, December 2002

# OH BABY!

# Amazing Baby Animals

by Kris Hirschmann

SCHOLASTIC INC.

New York   Toronto   London   Auckland   Sydney
Mexico City   New Delhi   Hong Kong   Buenos Aires

# We're going ape over our new baby!

**Weight at birth:** 4 pounds

**Eyes:** Dark brown

**Fur:** Brown-black all over

**Special features:** Flat nose with two big nostrils; hairless, dark-skinned face; strong, grasping hands and feet

**Comments:** Mommy loves carrying her little baby! She holds the infant in her arms and takes him everywhere she goes.

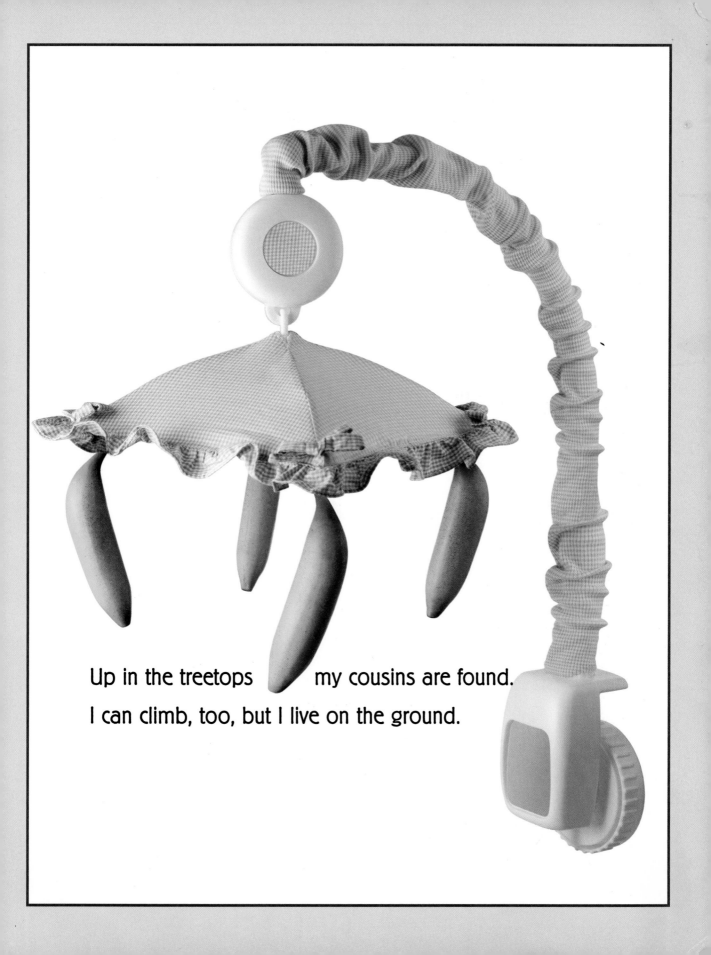

Up in the treetops        my cousins are found.

I can climb, too, but I live on the ground.

# Western Lowland Gorilla

A baby gorilla is carried by its mother for the first three months of its life. When the baby gets strong enough, it begins riding on its mother's back instead. A young gorilla will cling to its mother until it is three to four years old.

# Activity

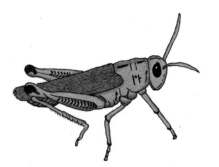
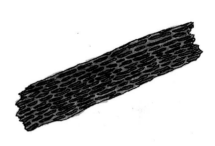

## What's for Dinner?

In the wild, gorillas are herbivores. This means they eat only plants. Can you point at the foods a gorilla might eat?

*Answers:*
*A gorilla might eat leaves and bark.*
*A gorilla would not eat a bug, a mouse, or a bird.*

# Did you hear about our baby?

| | |
|---|---|
| **Weight at birth:** | 40 pounds |
| **Eyes:** | Big, wide, and dark |
| **Hide:** | Brown body; white-and-black-striped legs with white stockings above the hooves; tan patch on the chest; white face |
| **Special features:** | Large, flexible ears; long black tongue; tufted tail |
| **Comments:** | Baby is a fast learner! She was able to stand on her own four legs just 30 minutes after she was born. |

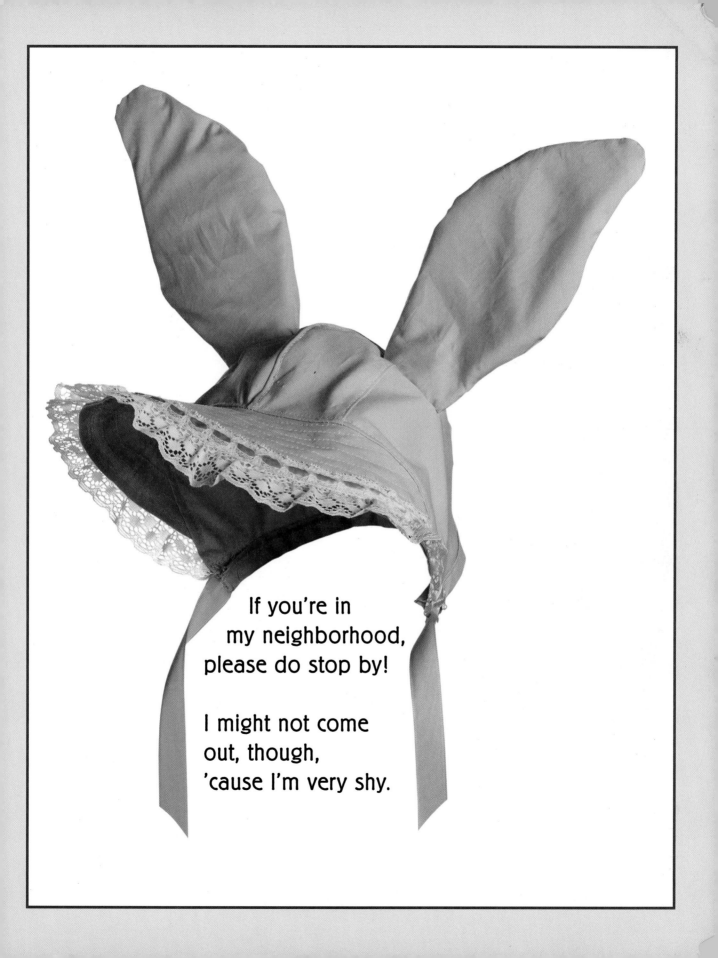

If you're in
my neighborhood,
please do stop by!

I might not come
out, though,
'cause I'm very shy.

# Okapi

Okapis are shy animals that like to stay hidden. Their many-colored hides blend into the shadows of their forest home. A baby okapi stays with its mother for about a year and then leaves home when it gets big enough to take care of itself.

# Activity

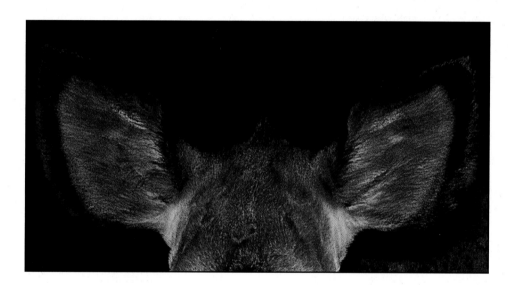

## Hear, Hear

Big ears help animals hear better. A large ear is able to catch more sound waves.

Cup one hand behind each of your ears to give yourself "okapi ears." Do things sound louder?

# Eight new toes for us to tickle!

**Weight at birth:** 1.5 ounces

**Eyes:** Small, dark, and beady

**Feathers:** Brown, with a white rump and belly

**Special features:** Sharp, curved beak
Long, skinny legs
Two strong wings

**Comments:** We think baby will grow up to be bright red all over—just like her mommy and daddy!

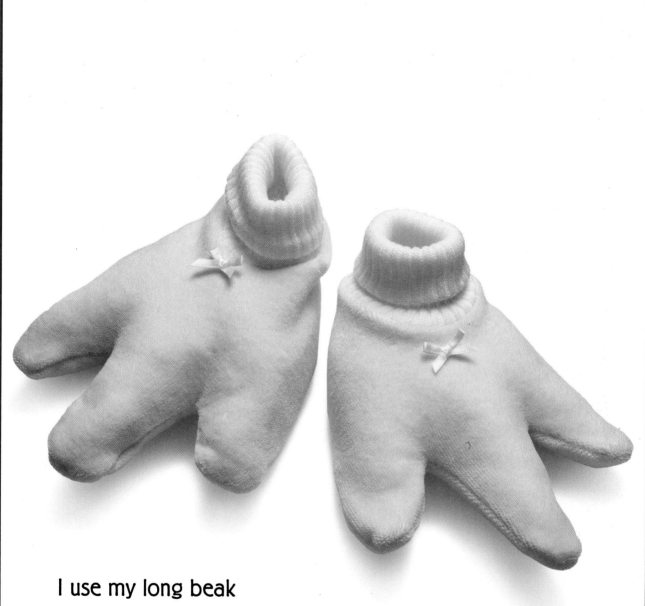

I use my long beak
to pluck food from the sea.

Shrimps, crabs, and fishes
are tasty to me!

# Scarlet Ibis

A female scarlet ibis lays two or three eggs at a time. Both parents guard the eggs until they hatch. The baby birds grow feathers soon after they hatch. In about four weeks, the babies will be able to fly!

# Activity

## Footprints in the Sand

Scarlet ibises have four long toes on each foot. Three of the toes point forward, and one points backward.

You can make a scarlet ibis footprint stamp! Use a blunt knife to cut a potato in half. Have an adult help you with this.

Then remove potato around a footprint shape like this:

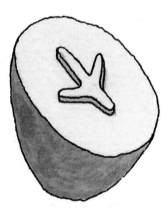

Press the finished stamp against an ink pad. Then press the inky stamp against a piece of paper to leave a perfect footprint.

# Introducing our little nipper!

**Length at birth:**     7 inches

**Eyes:**     Light brown with vertical slit pupils

**Skin:**     Many shades of brown; armor plated with lots of large, tough scales all over

**Special features:**     Eighty sharp teeth; strong jaws; thick, spiky tail

**Comments:**     We love our baby's cute little upturned nose!

You'll stay far away
from my mouth
if you're wise.

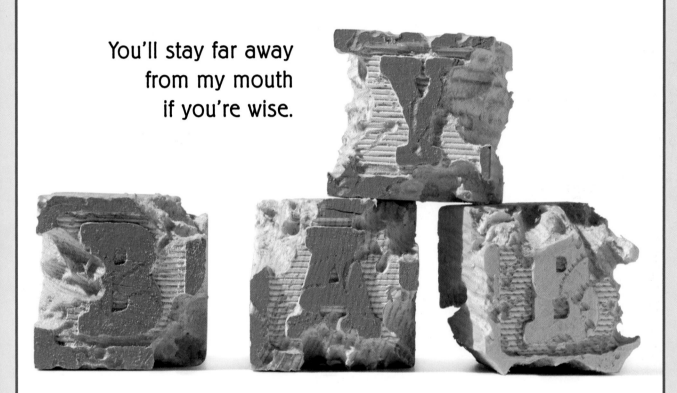

My sharp teeth can hurt you
despite my small size.

# Dwarf Caiman

Dwarf caimans are the smallest members of the crocodile family. These reptiles lay eggs in mounds and guard them until they hatch. Then the mother caiman protects the babies until they are large enough to defend themselves.

# Activity

## Tons of Teeth

Caimans are predators, which means they hunt and eat other animals. They have lots of sharp teeth that help them hold on to their prey.

Compare the caiman jaw to the human jaw.

 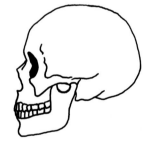

Which has more teeth?

# Our new baby is a ton of fun!

| | |
|---|---|
| **Weight at birth:** | 150 pounds |
| **Eyes:** | Squinty, surrounded by wrinkly skin |
| **Skin:** | Leathery and gray all over, with many thick folds |
| **Special features:** | Four broad hooves with three toes each; bumpy knobs all over skin; two perky ears |
| **Comments:** | Daddy weighs 6,000 pounds. We hope our baby grows up to be just as big and strong as his father! |

There's one tiny bump on my nose when I'm born.
That bump will grow into a long, pointy horn!

# Indian Rhinoceros

Most rhinos have two horns. But the Indian rhinoceros has just one. This sharp horn is made from the same material as hair and fingernails. Baby rhinos stay with their mothers until they are three years old. Then they leave to go live by themselves.

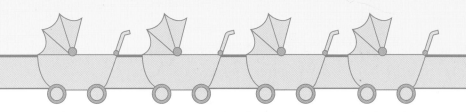

# Activity

## Rhino vs. Human

Rhinos are the second largest land mammals. Only elephants are heavier.

How many 200-pound adult humans would it take to balance one 4,000-pound rhinoceros?

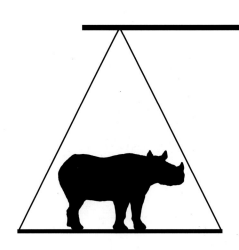 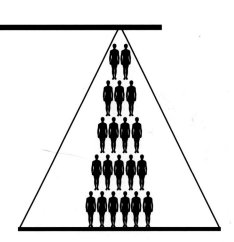

# Come monkey around with our new baby!

**Weight at birth:** 14 ounces

**Eyes:** Brown

**Fur:** Bright orange on most of the body, white around the face

**Special features:** Long, thin, flexible tail
Two big, hairless ears
Squeaky voice

**Comments:** Our baby is already using her tail to balance on branches. She'll be able to scramble through the treetops in no time at all!

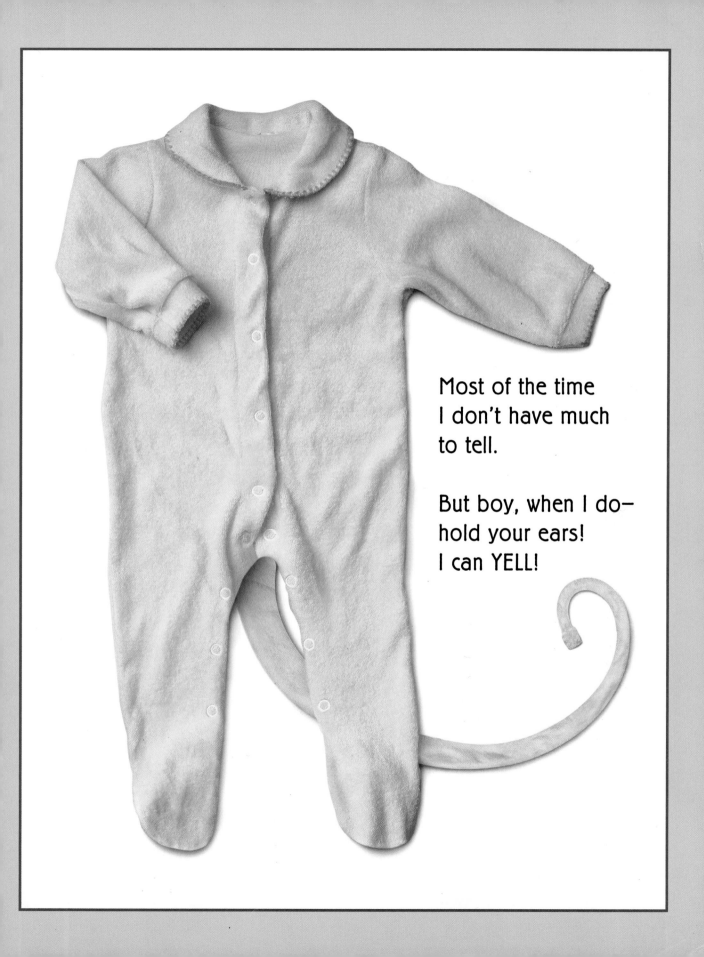

Most of the time
I don't have much
to tell.

But boy, when I do—
hold your ears!
I can YELL!

# Silver Leaf Langur

Adult silver leaf langurs have dark fur. A baby, however, is bright orange when it is born. The baby's colorful fur makes it easy for the grown-up monkeys to spot. As the baby grows up, its fur and skin will get darker.

# Activity

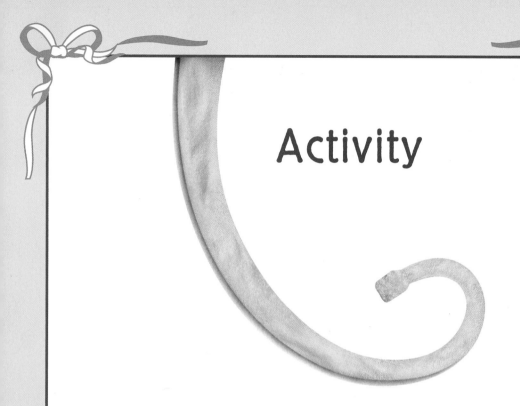

## Balancing Act

Silver leaf langurs use their long tails for balance. Balance is very important when you live in a tree!

You can see for yourself how a tail provides balance. Stand on one foot without touching anything. It's hard!

Now stand on one foot again. But this time, touch a wall with the fingertips of one hand. Do you feel how much easier it is to balance?

Your arm steadies you. That's how the silver leaf langur's tail works, too.

# Look who just slithered into our lives!

| | |
|---|---|
| **Length at birth:** | 10 inches |
| **Eyes:** | Round, small, and dark |
| **Scales:** | Gray, yellow, brown, and black |
| **Special features:** | Two sharp fangs; flickering tongue; skin "hood" that opens around the neck |
| **Comments:** | Baby likes to eat frogs and toads. He can catch them all by himself! |

Most people don't like me.
I give them a fright!

They know I can kill them
with one deadly bite.

# Egyptian Cobra

When an Egyptian cobra thinks it will be attacked, it raises the front part of its body and opens skin flaps on its neck to form a "hood." When the hood is open—watch out! This snake may bite. Its venom can kill a person in just 15 minutes.

# Activity

## Coiled Snake

When snakes rest, they curl their long bodies into tight coils. You can make a coiled snake that turns around and around!

Draw a spiral like this one on a piece of thin cardboard. Cut along the lines. Have an adult help you with this.

Decorate your snake any way you like.

Poke a hole in the head and tie a piece of string through the hole.

Now hang your coiled snake anywhere you want. Watch it spin!

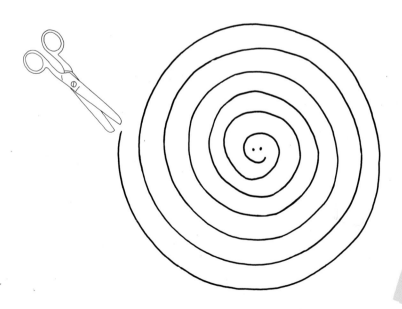

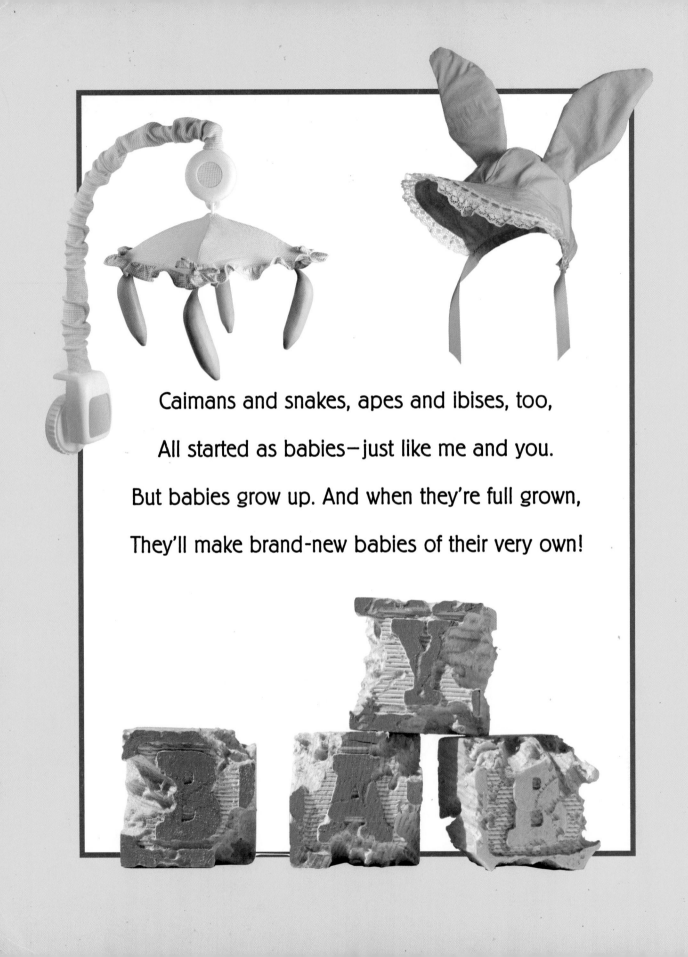

Caimans and snakes, apes and ibises, too,

All started as babies—just like me and you.

But babies grow up. And when they're full grown,

They'll make brand-new babies of their very own!